Björn Hróarsson & Malcolm Holloway

Iceland

– Colours of the Rainbow –

Pjaxi ehf.

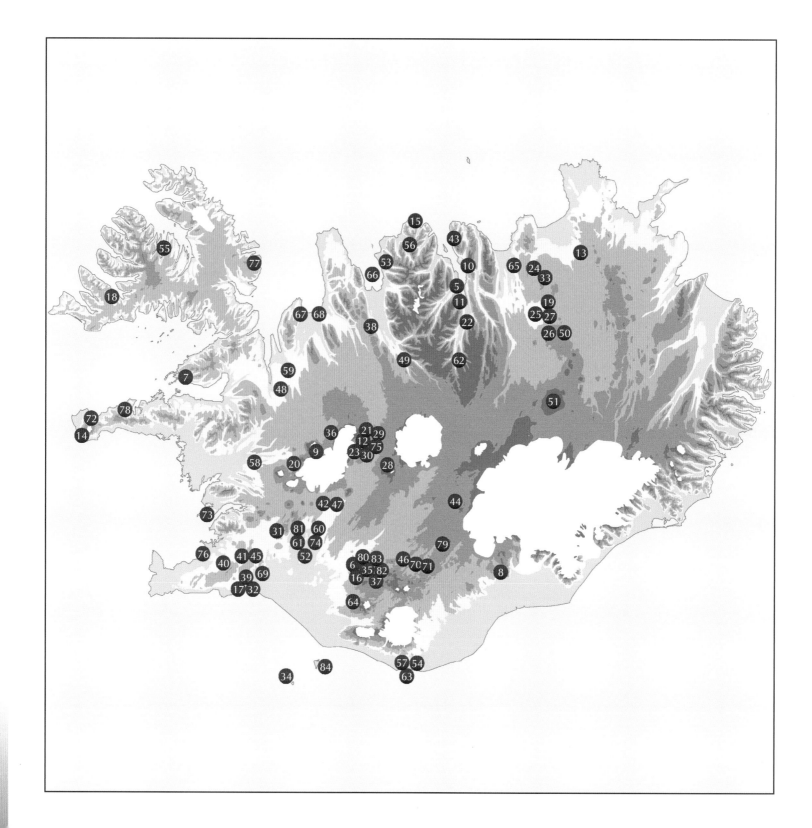

CONTENTS

Iceland – Colours of the Rainbow –

© Björn Hróarsson
© Malcolm Holloway

Design & layout
Pjaxi ehf.

Printing
Pjaxi ehf. / Delo tiskarna, Slowenia.

Photography
Björn Hróarsson

Pjaxi ehf. 2004

ISBN: 9979-783-09-5

The Icelandic landscape is a unique and ever changing picture.

A forbidding view of grey moorland can quickly become one of gently rolling, richly coloured countryside as the storm clouds move on and the sun breaks through. Passing showers add a glistening sheen to verdant pastureland. A rainbow arching over the scene invites you to pass through and find untold natural treasures.

This book will occasionally take you to popular places, visited by large numbers of people every day. It will also give you a glimpse of many less well-known gems created by nature – places that escape the attention of most of us, even though they are just a short distance from busy roads and crowded sites of interest.

The book begins with a number of pictures showing bright colours that stand out against the Icelandic landscape. But a closer look will show that the later pictures are arranged to show off the subtly changing hues of the countryside – golden yellows, verdant greens, eye-catching reds and cool blues.

Join us as we pass beyond the rainbow in search of natural wonders in this land of ever-changing colour.

In the early evening of 26th February, 2000, a series of earth-tremors were detected in the area of Mt. Hekla, Iceland's most notorious volcano. An eruption began a few hours later. The winter weather made travel difficult and only few people managed to reach the area before activity subsided on the 8th March.

The eruption had lasted just 11 days and had been at its most powerful during the first 24 hours. However, a wide fan of lava spread over an area of 18 km^2.

On 2nd April, a party of enthusiasts gathered and made their way onto the mountain. The picture shows the brightly coloured group on the lip of a crater above the new lava field. Clouds of steam belched periodically from the hot fissure, reducing visibility to less than one meter, obscuring the next man despite his vivid outer layer. The group moved onward or photographed the scene as the air cleared between the passing of each steamy cloud.

Snæfellsnes is a long arm of land stretching out into the Atlantic Ocean, about an hour's drive north from Reykjavík. To the north of Snæfellsnes there is a wide, relatively shallow bay called Breiðarfjördur, the Broad Fjord. There are farmsteads dotted all around the coast and also on some of the islands in the fjord, although few of them are now inhabited all year round.

The farm in this picture is quite typical and you can see the original house in the centre, with its low stone walls, timber frame and turf roof. Houses such as this were used in many places well into the 20th century, until the development of the road system gave access to concrete and other more modern building materials.

This is a common rural scene with red roofs standing out against the blue sky. However, the buttercups in the pasture tell us that some years have passed since livestock grazed here.

The main "crop" for this farmer, like many others in the area, is down from the eider ducks that nest in their thousands all along the shoreline. The birds build their nests in the grass, adding a cosy lining using small feathers they pluck from their breasts. Taking a portion of the down from the nests causes the birds no discomfort and in return, the eider ducks enjoy the protection of the farmer from predators. Many return to the same area year after year.

For almost 1,000 years, travel in Iceland meant a journey on foot, on horseback or by sea. The first motor vehicles had to contend with rough roads and tracks and even today, four-wheel-drive is often necessary for safe travel in country areas and in the highlands.

This is a Willys Jeep, manufactured in 1953. It is one of many such vehicles that were a common sight in the country-side from 1945–60. They were not only used for transport. Many were put to work in the fields during haymaking and other farming tasks. Like many others, this one has been adapted and it now has a custom built body – much more comfortable for the drive to the farmers' ball when the season's work is done!

Eiríksjökull is a table mountain (1,675 m), its summit covered with glacial ice that is now receding. As the ice melts and retreats up the slopes of the mountain, it leaves behind scarred rocks, mounds of loose stones that were scraped up as the icy tongues of the glacier moved to and fro and in some places it deposits a thick layer of glacial mud. The thin surface crust might support the weight of a man, but even the best equipped all-terrain vehicles grind to a halt as they sink deeper and lose their grip.

The members of this rescue team were on a training expedition when they found themselves in need of assistance. Luckily, the extra traction of the white jeep, pulling from the edge of the muddy area, was enough to rescue the rescuers.

The autumn weather brings a beautiful, golden-red colour to the moors but it also brings storms that herald the approach of the cold winter season. There is a heavy shower sweeping down the valley from Fjörður in the north of the country. There were a number of farms in this remote valley until the 1940s supporting several families, but now they are all uninhabited.

Akureyri, in the north of Iceland, is the country's second largest town. Residents might tell you that the weather was good last summer – on both days! The summer day shown in this picture was not one of them as a series of showers swept up the fjord Eyjafjörður, dousing the town at regular intervals.

Showery weather is often accompanied by one of nature's most colourful phenomena – the rainbow – compensation for the greyness we have to endure as the low clouds pass overhead.

Most volcanic activity in Iceland occurs in a broad band that curves from the southwest of the island, up through the interior to the north. During the last 50 years there have been eruptions in the Westman Islands, Surtsey, Hekla, under Vatnajökull Glacier and at Krafla in the north.

There are in addition many hot areas where geothermal heat reaches the surface, affecting water and vegetation. One such area is Hveravellir, in the Central Highlands. A number of hot springs bubble to the surface and the mineral content of the water and the immediately surrounding ground gives them different hues. The simmering pools have names such as Red Spring, Blue Spring and Green Spring, amongst others.

This is Red Spring, situated in marshland on the southern edge of the geothermal area. It has changed somewhat in recent decades and its red colour is becoming more pronounced. The spring bubbles furiously at times and its surface may bulge up to half a metre, but it will not spout and produce a fountain like the famous Geysir, further to the south.

Rainbows are formed when the sun shines through water droplets in the atmosphere. The spray from waterfalls can cause the effect as well as rain. The Jökulsá á Fjöllum River flows for over 200 km in a northerly direction from Vatnajökull Glacier. For much of its length it has carved a rugged canyon in which is found Europe's most powerful waterfall – Dettifoss (44 m). This picture was taken in early winter when the water level was low, but a rainbow still adds its many colours to the scene.

At the western tip of Snæfellsnes there is an area of weird lava shapes and black sandy beaches known as Djúpalónssandur. It is a fascinating area at the foot of the volcano that has attracted many visitors over the centuries.

Muscular men and women who visit this spot are invited to test their strength by lifting each of a group of boulders of increasing weight. Sailors in a bygone age had to prove their power by lifting each of these stones in turn. The smallest of the original stones is now broken but three others (49 kg, 140 kg and 155 kg) remain. It is a notable achievement for a man to lift the largest, known as Full Strength, up onto his chest and place it on the stone table in front of him.

A rainbow curves in a low arc across the craggy horizon as a shower crosses the landscape lit by evening sunshine.

The low winter sun casts a red glow onto the clouds above the cold landscape. But some of the ground is not as cold as it might seem at first sight. This picture was taken in January, 1991, on the slopes of Mt. Hekla, shortly after an eruption. The dark patches in the foreground are ash deposits and the black band of rock in the centre of the picture is new lava, still hot enough to melt the snow that falls onto it.

Many people climb Mt. Hekla each year but it can be an equally satisfying experience walking around the foot of volcano at a lower level, although the terrain is not always easy. As evening approaches you can pitch your tent and enjoy the magnificent environment that nature has sculpted. Whichever route you take in this region, you will find weird and wonderful natural formations that will ensure an unforgettable experience.

At the same time as the Egyptian Pharaoh Cheops was building his pyramid near Giza, a powerful eruption occurred in a crater about 20 km east of the spot where Reykjavík now stands. The area is now called Bláfjöll or the Blue Mountains and it is a popular skiing centre.

Lava from the eruption spread over a vast area of 100 km². Under the lava, in the area close to the main crater, are a number of caves where nature has hidden some of her most fascinating creations. Thin strings of solidified lava hang from the roof of the caves and below them, reaching up from the rocky floor, metallic-blue stalagmites stand, each formed by the fusion of solidified lava droplets.

Stalactites and stalagmites are found in limestone caves in many parts of the world, formed by the action of water on the rock over years, decades or even centuries. These lava creations, however, were formed quickly as the magma cooled and they are the same age as the surrounding lava field. The picture shows a scene as old as the Cheops Pyramid that is surely just as much one of the wonders of the world.

Most of the sand around Iceland's shores has volcanic origins and it is black or grey. Arnarfjörður in the west, however, has an attractive golden beach. Light coloured beaches are usually formed from quartz sand but the beach you see here is made from the ground shells of molluscs, crabs and other shellfish.

A series of deep valleys run down to the sea along this coastline with high ridges between. A fugitive from Norway made his home in one of the valleys where he lived for some years.

However, his pursuers never gave up and they sailed to Iceland and found him. A group of 15 men wrought their vengeance one day when Hringur, the fugitive, was alone. He fought hard for his life but was eventually overcome by weight of numbers. The valley is called Hringdalur.

A sword was unearthed in 1863 and road construction workers uncovered another in 1950. Both weapons are preserved in the National Museum of Iceland. Whether or not they are connected to the death of Hringur is not known.

This is Námafjall, a short distance from Lake Mývatn in the north of the country. The area has seen volcanic activity in modern times with the Fires of Mývatn between 1724 and 1729 and the more recent Krafla eruptions that began shortly before Christmas, 1975 and lasted until September, 1984.

Geothermal heat reaches the surface on the higher slopes of the mountain, which is devoid of vegetation. The orange colours are the result of sulphur deposits and other minerals. The sulphur was mined and exported for several hundred years until the middle of the 19th century, leaving behind a scarred and barren hillside.

Caves under the lava have been put to use by men since their arrival in Iceland. The Hallmundarhraun lava field was formed in an eruption in the first decade of the 10th century and a number of caves have been discovered beneath its surface, some of which would have remained warm for many years with a comfortable room temperature all year round.

One cave contains a pile of old animal bones which are amongst the oldest relics found in Iceland. Most of the bones are from beef cattle and tests indicate that the animals were slaughtered around the year 940, just a few years after the formation of the lava field.

The bones formed a large heap but over the years, visitors have taken souvenirs and much of the original content of the cave has disappeared.

One story says that a group of outlaws lived in the cave and stole animals from the neighbourhood. Capturing the group was not easy as the cave was easily defended. However, the men were seized as they took a nap after a hard day's work on the mountain slopes rounding up their illegal catch.

Whatever the truth of this tale, it is clear that the residents of the cave moved to a new location when the lava cooled and the temperature in the caves fell.

Geothermal areas remain active for decades or even centuries. Rain water seeps through the ground and comes into contact with hot rock. It heats up and may even boil. Steam then forces its way to the surface and sulphur and silicon build up around the vents, creating a delicate crust.

Grund is an ancient manor some 20 km inland from Akureyri. Early one November morning in 1905 a crowd of 800 people made its way to the settlement where a new church was to be consecrated. Building work had been completed the day before and the entire throng squeezed into the church though there was certainly not enough seating for everyone. A three-coloured flag flew from the tower, the colours green, white and blue depicting the earth, the ice and the sky.

The church is still much the same as it was on the day of its consecration. Magnús Sigurðsson, carpenter and seafarer, was the builder and he chose to ignore the tradition of aligning a church from east to west. The church at Grund has its altar at the north end and its main door to the south. Although some say this was more in keeping with the ancient lore of fairies and "hidden people," it is more likely that the intention was to shelter the entrance from the prevailing winds that whistle up the valley.

The timber for the church came to Akureyri by sea in the winter of 1903–4 and was moved from there to Grund by sledge and horse-drawn cart. Magnús later became the second person to import a motor vehicle into Iceland when he bought a truck to transport his equipment and materials.

The sun hangs just above the horizon casting a golden glow over the landscape. These pictures might have been taken around midnight in midsummer, or perhaps it was midday in the depths of winter?

The Icelandic mainland lies just outside the Arctic Circle. The sun rises every day, except in the shadow of high mountains or in deep, steep-sided fjords. Daylight hours are short in midwinter and the sun climbs just a few degrees above the horizon. However, during the summer months of June and July, the sun dips just below the horizon and reappears a short time later. Night and darkness are forgotten for several weeks.

Midwinter. Lake Mývatn is frozen and the weak winter sun reflects on the icy surface. The lake gets its name from the countless number of insects that breed, feed and develop in the shallow water – Midge Lake. Enormous swarms of the flying insects take to the air on calm summer days forming clouds above the banks and between the trees. They are harmless and do not usually bite humans.

The larvae live in the lake, some for up to two years, and as many as 200,000 or even more can be found in a single square metre on the bed of the lake.

However, during the winter there are few signs of life. Perhaps the tracks of an arctic fox, on a long trek foraging for food in the frozen landscape.

Some caves are warm as a result of volcanic activity but many are very cold. The temperature in this cave in the Mývatn area rarely rises above freezing point. The mound of ice is lit by a carbide lamp of a type that is popular with cave explorers.

A single cloud veils the sun for a minute or two. Winter storms can be violent but the tranquillity of a long, calm, summer evening is ample compensation. Steam from a geothermal area in Mývatn district drifts though the shadows.

Öskurhóll, or the Roaring Mound, is a 1-metre-high steam vent with a coating of silicon at Hveravellir in the centre of the country. Steam blows continuously from two holes on the top of the cone-shaped mound. It was given its name in 1752, when it had three holes. It whistled, rumbled and moaned with unceasing power.

Öskurhóll now hisses rather gently. The temperature at the opening is 97 degrees, almost the boiling point of water. Because of the height above sea-level at Hveravellir, water boils at 98 degrees, so it will take a little longer to cook your potatoes here than it will in Reykjavík, where water boils at 100 degrees.

When flowing lava follows the same course for a long period it forms lava channels that develop into tunnels below the solidified lava. Magma from the core of the volcano can run for long distances through these tunnels.

When activity dies down the remaining lava will sometimes run out of the tunnel, leaving an empty cave below the surface. There are many fascinating and unique formations in these caves.

Surtsey, the world's newest natural island, rose from the sea on the 15th November, 1963. It was an explosive eruption. As the magma poured from a fissure on the seafloor it was cooled instantly as it came into contact with the cold seawater. The island was formed as loose volcanic material and ash accumulated rapidly and finally broke the surface of the Atlantic Ocean a few kilometres off the south coast of Iceland.

Within three months the island had reached a height of 174 m above sea-level, 300 m above the seafloor. The eruption then moved to a crater on the west of the island that ejected lava until the summer of 1965.

Lava continued to run from other craters until June, 1967, at which time volcanic activity ended.

The picture was taken in one of the craters on the island. It was one of the last areas of activity. The hill in the background was formed from volcanic material ejected during the early weeks of the eruption.

Surtsey reached a maximum size of 2.7 km^2 but the perpetual action of the Atlantic rollers has eroded the new island and at the turn of the century it was only half that area.

The initial powerful phase of the 1991 eruption on the flanks of Hekla lasted just a few days but lava continued to flow from a new crater for over a year. Although the crater was formed from loose material and ash, it did not collapse at the end of volcanic activity, as often happens.

A team went out to investigate the area. The terrain is very rough and they waited until mid-winter, when a thick layer of snow made progress much easier.

The lava and the crater were hotter than expected when the team arrived, limiting the scope of their survey.

Once the snow melts and there is no thick blanket to protect the delicate environment, vehicles must keep to designated roads and tracks. However, in the remotest areas these tracks are often indistinct and their courses may only be approximately marked on maps.

This vehicle is the pride of the Hafnarfjörður Rescue Team, with power delivered to all six wheels. Progress is, all the same, slow. It takes around two hours to drive from Reykjavík to the inner end of Borgarfjörður. From there it is just 30 km to the team's final destination but it took over six hours to drive that distance – about the same time as it would take to walk the same route!

The mighty volcano Hekla erupted toward the end of February 2000. Although bad weather was forecast, the attraction of seeing one of nature's most powerful and awe-inspiring phenomena was enough to draw many hardy people, and traffic streamed from Reykjavík in an easterly direction, hoping to arrive within two or three hours.

But the forecasters were right and the weather worsened, winter's icy fingers gripped the land, the wind grew strong and the falling snow was blown horizontally across the landscape.

Those who had set off early were rewarded with sights of red hot magma as it was ejected from craters on the flanks of the mountainside. Molten lava ran down the slopes, glowing in the dim winter light.

But many unfortunate people were caught in traffic jams that finally ground to a halt as the roads became impassable.

While some will remember the eruption of 2000 as a demonstration of the power of nature as awesome volcanic energy was released, others will have memories of a different face of nature, as they spent the night trapped in their vehicles watching the snowdrifts build up all around them.

Skagafjörður is in the northwest of Iceland. One of its more unusual resources, an unexpected bonus from the sea, is driftwood. This is not flotsam and jetsam from wrecks or passing ships. Every year, whole logs and tree-trunks are washed up onto the shore in their thousands, having been carried by ocean currents from tree-felling operations in the forests of Northern Russia.

Víðimýri is a small farming community near the coast that has existed since the very early days of the settlement of Iceland. A church was built soon after Iceland's conversion to Christianity and services are held there to this day. It has been rebuilt several times over the centuries and in 1834, a new building was erected using driftwood topped with a turf roof.

This wooden structure lasted for over a century but in 1936 the parishioners decided to pull it down and build a concrete structure. The government stepped in and financed a comprehensive refurbishment so that the wooden church could be preserved for the nation.

The interior is intact and contains many artefacts from the 18th century built by skilled craftsmen of the period. The pulpit is thought to be older and was carefully preserved when the church was rebuilt.

The material ejected from volcanoes varies in size from minute grains of ash, sand, cinders and boulders to gigantic blocks the size of buildings. Very often the material fuses to form mounds, hills or mountains of soft, crumbly rock. Sometimes the mounds or craters are just heaps of loose pieces that are often very colourful.

The attractive colours of the red cinders have proved irresistible in recent years and whole hillsides have been excavated to provide material for red gravel driveways and footpaths.

The lava formations here and on the opposite page were found in caves not far from Reykjavík. These "rows of teeth" are in the Bláfjöll district and in the lava field close to Hafnarfjörður.

These delicate fingers of solidified lava and even more delicate strings hanging from the rocks were formed about 2500 years ago. These geological treasures are so sensitive that access to the area is allowed only for research purposes.

All around the country, both inland and on the coast, you will see distinctive red emergency huts. They are provided for sailors who make it to shore after their ships are wrecked, or for travellers caught in bad weather as they cross the lonely moors. Modern communications mean this network of shelters is now used less often but they are still a necessity in remote areas.

This hut is on the shores of Látraströnd in Eyjafjörður in the north of the country. It is built on the site of an old farmstead that was abandoned in 1943. There is no road and the rough track is only suitable for passage on foot or on horseback.

When a succession of winter storms has passed over and a thick layer of snow covers the ground, the countryside opens up once more for travel – maybe in a well equipped all-terrain vehicle, or on a motorised sledge, or perhaps on simple cross-country skis.

You will get a tan in clear winter sunshine just as quickly as on a Mediterranean beach in summertime.

On the surface, lava is often a dull, dark, grey colour even before it gains a coating of lichen. Below the surface, the story is different. This lava has an unusually high iron content and these walls have a distinctive rusty colour.

The journey from Reykjavík to Akureyri usually takes around 5 hours and many travellers stop at one of the service areas at Brú or at Staðarskáli. Between these two refreshment centres there is a large bridge under which passes a rather small river.

The source of the river is some 20 km to the south and a walk along its banks passes through delightful but deserted countryside. A few kilometres from the bridge, the weed-filled river turns green – a sure sign that there is hot water in the area.

Further upstream there are a number of hot springs. Some are on the banks and others are in the river bed itself. Walkers can bathe their weary feet in a hot pool or even take the plunge and sit one of two comfortably heated hot-pots provided by Mother Nature.

Small streams find a meandering path through the moors, eventually joining together to form larger rivers with crystal clear water. The glacial rivers carry a lot of very fine granules and the water looks grey and murky.

When rivers of each type meet the waters may not mix together for many kilometres. A band of clear water follows one bank, while on the opposite side the water is completely opaque.

As the thermometer rises and falls around freezing point, the continuous action of thawing and freezing produces all sorts of ice formations. Icicles hang where melted water trickles down and icy stalagmites reach up to meet them where the droplets fall to the ground.

Askja is a large, active volcano in the highlands. It erupted last in 1961, but in 1875 there was a massive explosive eruption which resulted in the ejection of enormous quantities of ash and other material. The magma chamber beneath the volcano quickly emptied and then collapsed, forming a deep crater. Over the following years it filled with water and the crater now contains the country's deepest lake. Ice covers the clear water well into the summer months.

Skálholt has been a religious centre for almost a thousand years and was the seat of 44 bishops from 1056 to 1801. Eleven churches have stood on the site, all on the same spot. Some were large and magnificent and the church that was built here in the 12th century was probably the largest church ever built in Iceland. It burned down in 1309 when it was struck by lightning.

Below the church there is a crypt and a secret underground passage leads to the schoolhouse and the residential houses that stand close by. It was used as a means of escape during some of the troubled periods of church history. Parts of the tunnel were ripped up and the building materials were sold in 1785, but it was restored in 1958.

This is the church of Gröf, near Hofsós in Skagafjörður. There was once a manor house here and a bustling community, though little evidence of them can be seen today. The church was built between 1670 and 1680 and it is one of the oldest in the country.

The church fell into disuse in 1765 but the building remained intact. It was used as a storage house for many years until it was reconsecrated in 1953. It is now preserved for the nation.

Hrossafoss falls in a narrow stream into a steep-sided basin. There are three small caves carved into the walls of the gorge, for the most part man-made. There are stories that tell of an Irish monk who lived in one of the caves before the first settlers came from Norway in 874. Recent research, however, suggests that the tales, describing monks and other religious followers from Ireland who lived in Iceland before the Vikings arrived, are fabrications from the early 20th century.

Water tumbles down mountainsides all around the country. It is pure and fresh and quite safe to drink. In rural areas, water is often simply piped from a mountain stream directly to the farm-house. This typical little waterfall is on the flanks of Fossahlíð in the Western Fjords.

Iceland's most powerful rivers have their origins under the glacial ice but between these torrents of murky grey water there are hundreds of smaller rivers and streams meandering down to the sea.

Salmon, trout and Arctic char abound in the crystal clear water, feeding mainly on insects that spend most of their lives on riverbeds or lake-floors. The surrounding wetlands are home to many species of birds.

An occasional fox might creep across the landscape and steal eggs or young from nests on the ground, but in recent years a new, unwanted predator has appeared on the scene. Mink, imported some years ago and bred for their fur, have escaped into the wild and are establishing themselves along riverbanks. They are voracious hunters and in some areas they are beginning to affect both bird and fish life.

This is the southernmost farm in the country at Reynishverfi. Large areas of South Iceland are covered in layers of black sand, the result of eruptions on land or under the glaciers. The sand was washed down in rivers or in floods that inevitably follow sub-glacial eruptions.

The farmers work hard to maintain their hayfields so that they can produce enough fodder for their livestock to see them through the lean winter months. The animals are kept away from the pastures during the summer and released onto the hillsides.

The car park on the left of the picture is for visitors to the coast, which is just a short walk from here. The coastline has many basalt formations with hexagonal rock columns and natural pavements.

The Icelandic Sagas are amongst the oldest written stories in the western world. They tell tales of life in Viking times. Many of the sagas are based on the lives and adventures of early Icelandic settlers, while others are mainly works of fiction.

The most celebrated writer of these long and detailed stories was Snorri Snorrason, who was born in 1178 and died over 60 years later, like many of the heroes and villains in his stories, at the hands of a murderer.

Snorri is said to have built this hot pool and it is thus one of the oldest man-made structures in Iceland. Hot water is channelled to the pool from a hot spring, along a 120-m-long underground culvert. Men have sought relaxation and recreation in the pool over the centuries, and maybe Snorri came here for inspiration as he lay in the clear, warm water.

Snorralaug, as it is known in Icelandic, is at Reykholt, Borgarfjörður, around two hours' drive from Reykjavík.

In Vatnsdalur, in NW Iceland, there is a deep pit of cold water called Kattarauga – Cat's Eye. Two natural floating islands drift on the surface, pushed from bank to bank by the force of the wind.

This jewel of nature gets its name from the glittering light that can be seen deep in the water when the weather is calm and the sun shines brightly.

One of the most popular locations in the Icelandic countryside is Gullfoss, the Golden Falls, a waterfall where Hvítá – the White River – tumbles over two high steps and drops 30 m into a dark narrow canyon. Below the falls, the river flows for several kilometres in a narrow gorge flanked by high cliffs.

The best way to see the spectacular scenery is to take a raft ride down the fast flowing river. Spray and waves might soak passengers in the rapids but expert rafters steer the boats, keeping them away from serious dangers.

Trees do not grow very high in Iceland. Winter temperatures are not very low compared to those in other countries at a similar latitude, but neither are summer temperatures very high and the rate of growth is very slow. Only a few hardy types survive in the low average temperatures.

Great efforts are being made to restore the forests that once covered most of the coastal plains and reached up onto the highlands.

Man has needed fuel over the centuries and the forests, the only source, were relentlessly felled during the early centuries of settlement. Flocks of sheep grazed on the newly cleared land and new trees could not establish themselves. In extreme cases this lead to erosion of the unstable soil and the creation of "dustbowls".

As more and more people build country cottages they are encouraged to plant trees, and forests are slowly reappearing on the landscape although the indigenous species take decades to establish themselves.

Although it is true that previous generations allowed their flocks to denude large swathes of land, for centuries the humble sheep provided the Icelandic nation with both food and clothing.

Plant life in the highlands of Iceland is quick to take root along the fringes of streams that find a route across the otherwise barren landscape.

The Reynisdrangar needles are just off the southernmost point of the mainland. Legend says that they were formed when two trolls were trying to drag a three-masted ship to land but they were caught in the early morning sunlight and turned to stone.

Hjalti Jónsson was born close by in 1869. At the age of seven he was climbing the cliffs along the coast in search of eggs, and at the age of eight he got to places beyond the reach of all who had tried before. A few years later he stood on the pinnacle of the needle on the extreme right of the picture, similar in height to the tower of Hallgrímskirkja in central Reykjavík. The climb was not easy and it took him 4 hours!

These turf-roofed huts are part of a settlement at Keldur, in the south of the country, which includes the oldest buildings in Iceland, dating from the 12th century. The two outlying huts are not quite so old and are in the middle of the modern farmer's hayfield.

Haymaking has always been an important part of rural life. Cattle, sheep and most horses are kept indoors during the winter months when they would have difficulty finding fodder. A good store of hay needs to be laid down in the summertime to provide for the animals through the cold season.

Reykur means smoke and it is common in place names. Reykjavík could be translated as "Smokey Bay". On a calm day you can see white clouds rising from geothermal areas all over the country. They are clouds of steam rather than smoke.

The source of the steam might be man-made, where boreholes have been sunk to exploit the natural heat. It may be a product of nature where the temperature close to the surface is hot enough to cause water to boil and form bubbling hot springs.

In a few cases, it could be a trail of steam left by a jet of boiling water that spouts explosively, high into the air – like the world famous Geysir, from which the word geyser is derived.

The picture shows the cloud left behind by a geyser in North Iceland. Ystihver is one of a number of geysers in a small area of geothermal activity beside the road that runs between Húsavík and Mývatn. It needs a little encouragement to show itself. If a few kilograms of soap-powder are emptied into the water the geyser will spout up to 30 m into the air after a short wait of a minute or two. A second showing often occurs 10–20 minutes later when the bowl has refilled.

The sheer cliffs of Drangey rise out of the sea in Skagafjörður, in northwest Iceland.

Over 200,000 birds have colonised the island and in past centuries a huge number of eggs were taken each year in springtime.

The rocky needle on the right of the picture is Kerling – the Old Woman. There was once a second needle – the Old Man – but it toppled into the sea in an earthquake in 1755.

Grettir is a notorious character from the sagas. He was one of two brothers who moved out to the island in 1028 when they were banished for crimes they had committed. After a few weeks, their fire died and Grettir swam to shore in search of a new source so he could rekindle the flames. This remarkable achievement is re-enacted from time to time by hardy souls who brave the cold sea and swim from the island to the mainland.

Hvítserkur stands in the sea close to Vatnsnes in Húnafjörður, in the northwest. It is 15 m high and populated by seabirds. Their droppings have given the rock its colour.

The sagas say that a troll who was passing through the district was caught in the sunlight and turned to stone. However, it is easier to imagine that this is some strange sea monster taking a drink from the salty water.

Erosion by wind and waves is a constant threat to this feature and its foundations have been strengthened in recent years to prevent it falling into the sea.

A church was built at Þingeyrar, near to Húnafjörður, in the years immediately after Iceland's conversion to Christianity and a monastery was established in 1133, the first in the country. This place was the seat of knowledge and learning in Iceland for many centuries and many ancient manuscripts that were written there have survived and are now preserved.

In 1860, the local Member of Parliament decided to replace the turf-roofed church with a grandiose new stone building. However, there was no stone in the area and all the materials had to be transported from other districts. Despite this, work began in the winter of 1864 and the stone was brought across the frozen estuary on horse-drawn sledges and dragged the final few hundred metres by teams of oxen. It took thirteen years until building work was completed but the church stands sturdy to this day.

A thousand golden stars are fixed to the ceiling. The pulpit was given to the church in 1696 and probably came from Holland.

Selfoss is a small market town in South Iceland. The church stands on the bank of the River Ölfusá, just above the estuary. It was completed in 1956.

The river is the biggest in the country with a water catchment area of over 6,000 km². It has burst its banks on three occasions in the last 100 years, causing considerable damage in the town.

In 1891, a suspension bridge was built on a spot close to the church. The bridge stood for more than fifty years until one day in 1944 two milk trucks drove across it at the same time. The supporting cables gave way under the weight, toppling the loaded trucks into the fast flowing current. The drivers were rescued and a new, sturdier suspension bridge was built on the same site.

When a blanket of snow covers the ground there are fewer colours on display but the pure white landscape is a pleasing to the eye and the bright daylight is uplifting.

Cross-country skis were once a necessity in rural areas but snowploughs, all-terrain vehicles and skidoos (motorised sledges) mean that mechanical transport is now available in almost all weathers.

However, cross-country skiing is now a recreational activity enjoyed by many. Some skiers choose to follow tracks that are laid in and around towns and villages or close to ski centres in the mountains. Others take to the open countryside or even make long journeys, pulling sledges behind them, loaded with supplies.

Cross-country ski boots clip into a fastening at the toe end and the heel is free, allowing a walking action. Travel across flat ground and on gentle slopes is easy but it takes a lot of practice to go up and down steeper hillsides.

Snæfellsjökull stands majestically at the end of the Snæfellsnes peninsula, reaching a height of 1,446 m. It is a volcanic cone, formed from countless eruptions from a single vent. The mountain is covered by a glacier with an area of 11 km². The last eruption is estimated to have taken place around the year 200, well before Iceland's first human inhabitants arrived.

It is not difficult to walk up the mountain. The slope is even and only becomes steep at the edges of the summit crater. However, the journey must be undertaken in springtime, before crevasses open and make the route dangerous or even impossible. Snow vehicles also carry passengers up to the summit. You can drive back down, or take your skis with you and enjoy what is probably the longest run in Iceland.

The heroes of Jules Verne's epic novel Journey to the Centre of the Earth begin their adventure on Snæfellsjökull descending a fictitious vent that takes them deep into the Earth's crust.

Snæfellsjökull is the highest mountain visible from Reykjavík.

Akranes is a town with a population of 5,500, across the bay from Reykjavík. It is one of the oldest habitations in Iceland.

A ferry used to sail between Akranes and the capital several times a day but a tunnel was opened in 1998 and the ferry was closed a short time later. The tunnel under the sea saves a long drive around Hvalfjörður. It is used by almost all traffic heading north out of Reykjavík.

This is Geysir's bowl, from which a steaming fountain spouts high into the air when the water in the underground chamber reaches temperatures above normal boiling point. The hot springs around the area appeared around the year 1300, but the geyser is thought to have come into existence after a powerful earthquake in 1640. It spouted a jet of water high into the air twice a day from then until the end of the 19th century, but activity then subsided.

Bláhver, the Blue Pool, is the largest of the hot springs in the Hveravellir area in the Central Highlands. It is 5 m in diameter and circular in shape. Occasional bubbles burst on the surface of the otherwise tranquil hot water.

The pool gets its blue shade from tiny crystals of silicon that form in the water, which is cooler than other springs, being around 90 degrees. This pool has hardly changed for the last 200 years. Descriptions from the early 19th century are equally fitting in the present day.

On a sunny day, the sea might look blue and inviting, but it is very cold. The Gulf Stream flows around the coast and keeps the temperature of the water above freezing, preventing ice from closing harbours during the winter. However, only a very few hardy souls take the plunge and risk swimming in the chilly water.

This Whooper Swan is taking advantage of a warm summer morning to take its young for a swim on the shore of Reykjafjörður á Ströndum, NW Iceland.

Swans are the largest of Iceland's birds. Many migrate to the northern British Isles for the winter but one in ten will spend the whole year in Iceland.

Nesting swans are found all over the country, both in the Highlands and on the coastal plain. They excavate a deep bowl in the ground and lay 4–6 eggs that hatch after about five weeks. The young hatchlings soon venture from the nest and take to the water. They generally learn to fly at around two months old. The cygnets follow their parents for a whole year until they are chased away when the next batch of eggs is due.

Swans keep the same mate for their entire lives and return to the same nest year after year. A single adult swan is a sad sight. It has almost certainly lost its mate and will remain a widow or widower for the rest of its life.

The fishing industry is the cornerstone of the Icelandic economy. All around the coast, wherever there is shelter from the Atlantic waves, there are harbours for the local fleet.

Until the last century, fishermen rowed out to sea in small groups, hoping to provide for their own communities. There are still many small boats operated by one or two men, but large factory ships produce catches all year round and the entire process of fishing, filleting, packaging and freezing is carried out on board.

The most commonly fished species are capelin, whiting, cod, herring and redfish. Most of the fish is exported, either frozen, dried and made into fish-meal or rendered down to make fish oil.

As the road network is extended and improved, more bridges are built. But there are still many places where the only way to the opposite bank is through the water.

Four-wheel-drive vehicles are safest but even ordinary cars can make a crossing if the bottom is firm and the water is not too deep. Crossing points are usually well marked and once you start there is no turning back. Speed is important – not so fast that the water comes over the front of the car. And no stopping!

This new lava flowed down the flanks of a crater formed during the Hekla eruption of 1991. News of the volcanic activity quickly spread and those who went to the area on the first night witnessed an amazing scene. The whole area was covered in winter snow and the temperature was many degrees below zero. Ice and snow made delicate, crystalline patterns on the rocks that glittered in the fiery orange glow of the vol-

cano. At the same time, a shimmering display of northern lights, the Aurora Borealis, danced across the night sky. Nature was showing some of her most spectacular phenomena.

Although this picture was taken three years later, in 1994, the lava was still hot enough to melt the snow and leave a black band showing on the white slopes of the snow-covered mountain.

This waterfall is sometimes called Mjólkurfoss – Milky Falls – because of its colour. The sun only shines on the falls early in the morning in high summer. The water cascades into a deep, gloomy chasm.

The ash column rises into the winter sky during the Hekla eruption of 2000. Southerly winds carried the ash across the highlands to the far north of the country, leaving grey deposits in the snow.

Iceland is an island. The first permanent settlers came from Norway sometime around the year 870. They found plenty of fish in the seas around the coast, rivers teeming with salmon and trout, enormous colonies of birds and a wild land where Mother Nature showed some of her more unusual tricks.

The settlers brought their sheep, cattle and horses, and the old breeds still roam the hillsides, graze the pastures or carry riders on their sturdy backs.

Over the centuries, the descendants of the Viking settlers and their entourage have developed into an independent, self-confident nation. Modern communications make distances seem shorter and travel is easier. After a millennium of isola-tion, Icelanders are now able to receive visitors and they are proud to show the world what a fascinating home nature has provided.

We hope this book has shown you some of the many facets of this unique land that nature has sculpted. If you have visited Iceland, then we hope you will feel tempted to return in the future. If you have not yet visited the Land of Ice and Fire then perhaps this book will help persuade you to make the journey to this island in the North Atlantic, and in the not too distant future you will stand on a glacier, or look over a lava field, or maybe relax in a pool of naturally heated hot water. Thank you for taking the time to read this book.